Studying Yourself

Maximize Your Potential while Avoiding Stress

James A. McCauley

Table of Contents

Introduction

Welcome to the Huddle! Thank you for joining this concise lesson. We are going to be discussing the benefits of studying yourself. Where do I start? There are so many benefits of studying yourself! We will be covering a few steps to take when doing so. Hopefully it leads to functioning on a fresh new level. My goal is to breed peace within you. Another goal is to help you learn more about yourself.

Conversation Focus

The intent of this book is to encourage us to study our lives. I want people to understand the advantages of doing so. I want people to walk away from this book and discover new levels of themselves. As a results, I plan to have readers feeling more confident and ready for what life throws at them. To become self-equipped. To inform you of the full potential within you. To become comfortable in your own skin.

Let's get started…

What do I mean by studying yourself? I'm talking about studying your actions, thoughts, words and more. Most of what I'm going to inspire you to do during your "investigation process" is to think to yourself. Process some simple thoughts within your mind. Coming to your own conclusion via your thoughts or actions based on your knowledge and experiences. It should be mind blowing. As you read this book and come across your findings remember this key principle:

"Everything happens for a reason."

Don't worry during your hard times. Don't remain in a slump. Remain positive and ready for more. Stay HUNGRY!

The following questions are examples of what I'm referring to when it comes to studying yourself. When going through this process, you're looking for the core reason to each. You may have an issue, negativity, or poor habit you want to look into. That would be wise on your part. Nothing like taking care of things that have the potential to hold you back from giving your max in life.

I like to reflect on the extraordinary fact that we are all uniquely made. We are 1 in 5 billion people. No one knows you better than you. That's the theme of this Huddle. Be you on purpose. Be comfortable in your own skin. I'm going to be presenting some questions that I want you to consider in your personal life. Find yourself and who you are. Possibly uproot character flaws and get rid of them for good.

Let's jump into the questions I promised you.

Self-Study Questions

Your Reaction

Why do you react in a negative manner when <blank> happens?
I'm convinced everyone has something that has the power to get them mad or put them in a sour mood. Maybe for you it's the thought of <blank> that just sends you over the top. The appearance of <blank> places you in an uproar.

What are you putting in the <blank>?

Why do you think you have unpleasant reactions?

What is the root of this issue?

Note: When you have an answer to the question(s) going forward, in order to dig deeper and grasp a better understanding keep asking "why?" until you reach the depth of the real true answer. As you continue to read keep in mind these questions are in place to get you started. You have the ultimate freedom to ask whatever you need to. Don't limit yourself. My infinite mind can only do but so much.

Is it only with this one situation that you react this way?
Do you have multiple things that get on your

nerves?

Do you let it get on your nerves to the point that you're unable to hold your anger in?

You may try to keep your anger to yourself but it just doesn't happen. You may release your anger in different ways, possibly yelling in an empty room, swinging in midair at nothing at all, or punching a hole in the closest wall, fellas. I say fellas, but you never know, there may be a few women punching holes in walls.

Your Mindset

Do you have a proper/positive attitude towards things that occur in your life?
Things that make people sad or upset but you on the other hand are able to remain reserved and chill. You've probably found yourself telling others you are the type of person who can let things slide by the wayside. You have no problem with most things other people would have a problem with. You are just that cool, calm and collective.

Do you have a negative attitude towards things that occur in your life?
Are you one of those people? People get tired of your presences because you are always complaining?

You are always complaining how life is not treating you fairly. You have this mindset that the world has you on its agenda, to ruin your specific day. You may use the phrase that "you can't get a break" a little too often.

Do you have a Godly approach to things?
It's good to be balanced in all things. With that being said you may understand that all things happen for a Gods good reason. You see the bigger picture! Gods' hand is in the midst of all situations. You believe God arranged everything to happen

under His control or final agreement. Feeling led to focus on the message from God versus the situation and how it makes you feel, etc. You have a God-Centered attitude. Remaining hopeful and ready to seek the underlining of the message. You believe you're being spiritually taught through occurrence you've come to know about.

Do you try to remain positive?
Do you make an effort to look at the glass half full? versus half empty? Ok that illustration has been over used over the years. Let's see...

Do you see that everything as a puzzle piece to Gods bigger picture? We are simply a piece of the puzzle. Things must occur for something else to occur. The ripple effect.

How can you remain positive at a difficult time? Challenge yourself to focus on God versus your circumstances. When you focus on God and his plans for you, you tend to feel significant and less significant at the same time.

Reflect on how many times God has used you to put a smile on someone face passing by. The person may have been having a depressing life and your one smile reminded them of the joy they once experienced. Your smile may have encouraged them to go and find that happy place again.

Just a thought: What is something you would share with someone in 30 seconds or less to sincerely express to them that taking their life isn't worth it?

Do you find yourself to be negative or positive when life throws a curve ball?
I was sharing something like this on social network. We have to be ready in and out of seasoning. Life is going to come at you. Life will get in your face and push you down! When this happens you have to remain firm in your hope in God and react the way that brings God honor. Life is testing you to see if you've passed the mark. Life is confirming if you a mature enough for the new blessings. God uses His creation (everything) to work together to build our encouragement. We have to soak up life principles and live by them versus, playing a victim all the time.

Your Surroundings

What is the one thing that has the power to make you mad the most?
The thought or the person that makes you upset. The site of whatever it is makes your heart race. It could be someone and not just something. When it's a person you may want to cause them harm with no regrets. Brain signals are sent to your face to quickly make a frowned up evil eyed face right away. You mentally get in position like the bull does when he sees the matador.

Do you allow situations to bring you down easily?
Are you the woe is me type of person, who is constantly finding ways to feel bad for yourself?

Do you look for sympathy?

Do you look for attention?

Do you lack being positive?

Do you have a hard time getting yourself out of a slump?

Are you able to fall into a slump at the first sign of defeat?
Is it easy for you to feel sad?

Are you a Debby Downer? I hope your name isn't first name Debby or Last name Downer. Ask your parents why they named you that?

Do you walk around with a frown on your face like you were born that way? Mean mugging everyone? Like you smell something terrible in the air?

Your Motivation

Are you hard on yourself?
Do you give yourself <u>any</u> credit? Not credit card!
But do you feel valuable?

When you fail at accomplishing the goal are you
your worst critic?

Are you your own "Mr. or Ms. I told you so"?
Asking yourself, "why did I even try, I know that
I'm not worth it." Telling yourself, "I knew I
couldn't accomplish this?"

Do you give yourself <u>enough</u> credit?
Most people primarily live off of the opinions of
others. Going in debt because they have to have
the best. They feel that if their friends have the
best, then they should to. Going in debt and getting
more and more blind to reality. Can't see their own
self-worth. Living off the energy people tell about
themselves. Trapped in the web of the world. You
are one of 5 billion people. You don't need anyone
to tell you who you are and to establish your self-
worth for you. You have something to offer the
entire world. I'm not pumping your head up. No,
this is true information. You are more valuable
than you can ever believe or imagine.

Are you self-motivated?

One of the best qualities you can have on your belt, is having self-motivation. Bosses love self-motivated employees. Most couples prefer their significant other to be self-motivated. It's a good habit to want more out of life. Living life to the fullest versus allowing life to live for you. That doesn't make sense. But it does when you reread the statement much slower. Go ahead, feel free to read again. I will be waiting at the next sentence.

Welcome back! Self-motivation takes you to the next level. When no one is there to push you over the edge. Not the cliff but over into a new level. Self-motivation pushes you out of your complacency zone. It fuels your brain and tells it to get off of its rear-end. Self-motivation revs the engine in the mind and gives it the needed gas to GO! Gas to launch forward.

When you lack self-motivation you have to be your own cheerleader. Yes, you read that right, your own cheerleader. You have to be your BIGGEST cheerleader. Can't have a ice cream sundae without the cherry. And the cherry on top of being self-motivated is being your <u>most loyal</u> cheerleader. You never let yourself forget about your dreams and what you desire to accomplish. You must be loyal to your dreams. You must aim each day to get closer to the goal. Self-motivation is at the core of any accomplished persons character.

Your Weakness

Do you let things catch you off guard?
Are you naive to things?

Do you expect the worst to occur all the time?

Are your prepared for what may come?

Do you live a life of training yourself to be prepared?

Never settle in life. Always ask yourself what could happen and assume the worst and prepare for the worst. If the worst never comes then guess what? You live another day! If a terrible situation comes around, guess what? You will be prepared! We call that #BEASTMODE! We're not throwing a naive party over here. Naw! We celebrating greatness!

You can neither be the fish or the shark. You can either be the one whom fears or you can be the one whom is feared. You can be the one who eats, or be the bait for the bigger fish, the choice is yours.

Do you work on improving your weaknesses?
When you are presented with your weakness,
what do you do?

Do you figure out some key things about how to
improve?

Do you fold in your imaginary shell?

Do you crawl in your bed and refuse to leave the
house?

Do you call on your mother to bail you out?

Do you stand firm with humility and work up a
plan to improve at your weakness?

Do you grab those flaws and make the most of
them? Admit your weakness and devote time to
creating good habits to make it a strength.

Do you know your weaknesses?
It's good to accept your weakness. I just heard an
addiction to drug commercial on the television
while typing the above paragraph. Reminds me of
the act of confession.

Confessing your weakness to yourself is 90% of
the battle. I'm guessing that percentage by the
way, along with all of the other people who toss
percentages out there. Side note: People act like
they have a percentage handbook in their back

pocket...I digress. Admitting your weakness is key. That sounds more realistic.

It's good to ask others about things they don't like about you. Ask them their view of things that you need to improve on. Ask someone that you confide in or trust. Confide, is an overused word these days. How about someone whom you may reach out to often? So when they tell you what you need to improve on, it's not an awkward pause with silence. Don't fear taking this step. You would be surprise, by taking this step may just lead to laughter and possibly a deeper respect level with them. You will most likely give them feedback. Don't start nothing and it won't be nothing!

Your Respect

Do you have respect for yourself?
Having respect for yourself shows up in your walk
and within your talk. Self-confidence breeds self-
respect.

Do you know the level of respect you get from
others?

Do you give respect to others or do you make them
earn it?

**Do you feel inadequate around certain people
or races?**
Do you feel inferior around certain people?

Do you feel less valuable when you enter a room of
people?

Are you comparing yourself to them too much?

Do you allow your view to lead to feeling out of
place?

Do you allow your thoughts to encourage you to
believe you're not worthy?

Without people looking in your direction or
speaking to you directly, do you mentally place

your self worth below theirs?

Do you say "That's just who I am?"
Insinuating that other people just need to deal
with you and your actions. Even if your actions are
good or bad it's not cool to just be living a life of
not caring what type of vibe you give off to others.
But on the other hand you care when they don't
give off the best vibe around you.

The Wrap Up

The previous questions are capable of pulling up some real issues for sure. They were mainly designed to guide you through your journey.

You're welcome to ask other questions in the same genre or if you feeling cocky then venture out from the subjects covered. As long as you are studying and better understanding yourself.

I care that you seek the core reasoning behind the hurdles and things holding you back from being the best you.

If need be, be sure to seek out more about your history. There may be something that you are unaware about that affects you. Genetic or generation trends within your family line. If you have the option to ask your parents some questions regarding your unknown history, I would definitely encourage you to do so. Parents have stories about us that we were simply too young to comprehend or remember.

Survey your fiends because of the influence they have on you. As you get older it's not easy to ditch some friends whom you have grew with. But if their negative influence is preventing you from performing at your max, then the answer is clear, it's time to ween them off.

Survey the people who are mostly around you. They may not be necessarily your friend but you associate with them often. Treat them like the discouraging friends. If they are holding you back in anyway consider weening them off as well.

Their influence shapes your outlook and encourage habits you may not have implemented or entertained without their introduction. You are their friend and/or associate the call is up to you. My advice is just that, advice! It doesn't take a genius to figure out avoiding negative people as much as possible is a good thing.

We have chapters in our life story. However, not all previous characters weren't designed to exist in upcoming chapters of our life story.

When you know the "why" to not so good situations in your life, you know what to look for. You see the signs coming. You have identified that particular issue. You will most likely be avoiding situations to increase unwanted scenarios.

Do you think this is going to be to much to ask of you? You are going to do fine! Don't sweat the small stuff.

Seek the reason why you may be shunning this opportunity versus trying it out or why you think it's too much to ask from you.

Have you ever quit anything?

Did you quit a job, a team, or your family?

Do you have trends in your life of being a quitter?

Seek out the reason "why" if this is you. When was the first time you quit something?

Why did you?

What satisfaction did you have?

What dissatisfaction did you have?

I ask questions all the time. It's something I was doing every day until I identified it as an essential mindset that benefit others. The goal is to teach you this habit of effectively studying yourself so you can live to the max with less stress. Naturally implementing these procedures throughout your day. Leading to a life understanding your abilities better.

This is the beginning of the journey. Review the questions within this book often to remain on your "A" game.

Stay tuned for more material regarding this topic of studying yourself. I'm also working on a book titled *Studying Others* which is magnificent and will be enriching for your life. I highly encourage you to get yourself a copy from the Amazon Kindle Store. Don't hoard all of this information for yourself, please share with friends and family members.

Self-study is a subject I love to talk and ponder about.

Best way to find my other books is to search "**HuddleTime**" in the amazon search field.

Thank you for joining me in the Huddle.
See you in the next book.

Thank you for your continued support.
James
01 September 2016